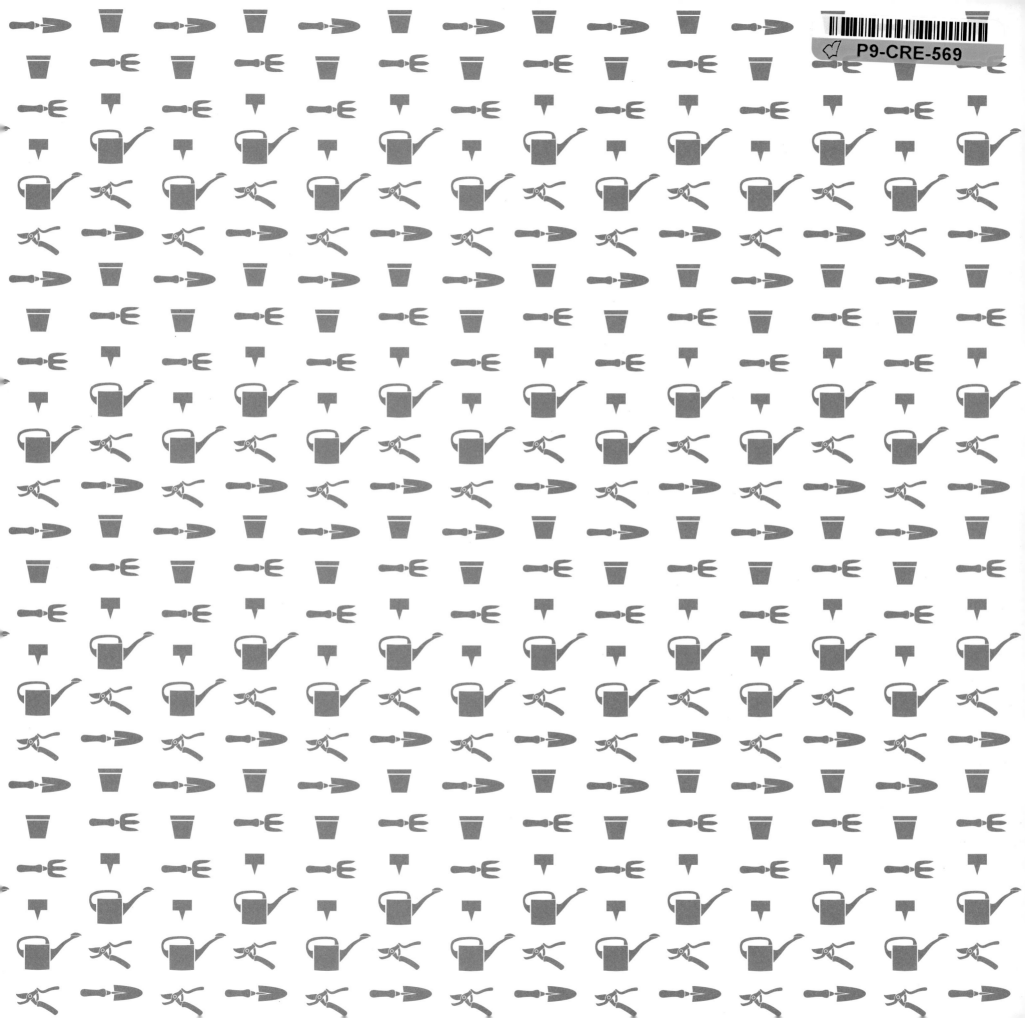

Start to plant

ROCK & ALPINE GARDENS

Create your ideal garden with these simple-to-follow projects

Graham A. Pavey

CHARTWELL
BOOKS, INC.

A QUINTET BOOK

Published by Chartwell Books
A Division of Book Sales, Inc.
114 Northfield Avenue
Edison, New Jersey 00837

This edition produced for sale in the U.S.A., its
territories and dependencies only.

ISBN 0-7858-0369-6

This book was designed and produced by
Quintet Publishing Limited
6 Blundell Street
London N7 9BH

Creative Director: Richard Dewing
Designer: James Lawrence
Project Editor: Diana Steedman
Editor: Janet Swarbrick
Photographer: Keith Waterton

Typeset in Great Britain by
Central Southern Typesetters, Eastbourne
Manufactured by Bright Arts (Singapore) Pte Ltd
Printed by Leefung-Asco Printers Ltd, China

AUTHOR'S ACKNOWLEDGMENTS

I would like to give special thanks to Dave, Jason, and Paul
of DJ Landscapes, Bromham, Beds., U.K.; to Stonemarkets,
Ryton on Dunsmore, Warwicks., U.K.; to Chas Bolton at
Wright's Builders Merchants, St Neots, Cambs.,U.K.; to
Sandra and Richard Oliver, Angela Whiting, Barry Johnson,
and all the staff at Anglia Alpines and Herbs Ltd,
Huntingdon, Cambs.,U.K.; and to Steve Woods and the staff
at Tacchi's Garden Scene, Huntingdon, Cambs.,U.K.

CONTENTS

INTRODUCTION

G rowing wild in the mountain ranges of the world are some of our loveliest garden plants – alpines. These rock and scree plants grow at high altitudes above the timberline, but the term "alpine" is loosely used to include a vast range of low-growing rock-garden plants, including many bulbs, that may be grown successfully at relatively low altitudes.

The term "alpine" also gives an indication of how we should grow these plants, but how we display them, like many other forms of gardening, changes as time passes. With today's more integrated approach to gardening, with more emphasis on the natural overall look of the whole garden, alpines and rock garden plants can be introduced into any size of garden to provide a wealth of beautiful species.

BILL SHAW

GRAHAM A PAVEY

Most are amenable and undemanding plants that will grow readily in a suitably prepared site in the garden. Not only rockeries, but areas of pebbles, stones, or cobblestones are attractive ways of growing alpines. Like cracks in paving and walls, they simulate wild conditions and allow the alpine or rock garden to become integrated into the overall design of the garden.

Rockeries are an excellent way of exploring the fascinating world of alpines. Even a tiny rock garden can accommodate many of these delightful plants, and different environments can be constructed to grow a range of species. Alpine plants are perfect for container gardening, and a miniature rock garden in a raised bed is an ideal option where space is limited. From sink gardens to hanging baskets, alpines can be used to create an all-year-round interest that is easy to maintain and requires minimum attention.

MATERIALS AND TECHNIQUES

Pea-size pebbles

Materials for Projects

Bricks come in a range of hardness, from very soft molded bricks to very hard engineering bricks. The softer the brick, the more prone it is to attack by frost, but it may have a more attractive texture than a harder one. Frost-damaged bricks can be a feature in themselves.

Cement is used for making hyper-tufa and for construction work.

Horticultural gravel is used as a mulch around plants in a finished rock garden. It keeps plants clean, and the soil cool and moist around plant roots.

Lean mix is a mix of 6 parts sand to 1 part of cement with the addition of a little water to damp it down slightly, making it easier to use. When laid, it will dry to make a solid base.

Pea-size pebbles are used for the surface of scree beds, as a mulch, and for lining the base of stone troughs. The grade should be no more than ½ inch in size.

Stone chips are small pieces of natural stone, used as an alternative to sandstone pebbles, river pebbles, or gravel where it might fit better with the local stone.

Crockery shards

Mulching mat

Tufa

Crockery shards provide drainage in the base of containers. They are usually broken flowerpots or tiles, but large stones or pebbles could be used.

A **mulching mat**, usually made from an openweave, man-made material, is useful for maintaining moisture in the ground and keeping weeds under control.

Tufa is a very light, unusual material. Despite its appearance, it is not a rock, but a limestone deposit laid down by water which has passed through limestone rock.

Types of Rock

When deciding what type of rock to use for a rock garden, the first choice should be indigenous stone, which will look more natural than anything else.

A visit to your local garden center will indicate which rocks are available.

Granite *is a very hard stone in a range of colors, depending on its original location. This shiny material looks out of place if used in a limestone or sandstone region.*

Sandstone *is a very soft material, not ideal for use in a rock garden because it tends to quickly disintegrate. However, if it is your local stone, then consider using it and replacing it when necessary.*

Limestone *is available in a wide range. Much of it is very soft and has a tendency to suffer frost damage, but there are a number of very hard limestones, for example "Purbeck," which are hard enough to use as paving stones.*

Yorkstone is a form of sandstone that makes a perfect paving material. It is also a good choice for rock outcrops and stone walls.

*Unusual **granite** egg-shaped and spherical stones are frequently dug out of gravel pits and tossed to one side. They are useful for creating attractive effects in a scree bed and flower border.*

Flint stones are useful, loosely laid, to create texture in a scree bed, or as an alternative to gravel around plants in a paved area.

Soil

Sharp sand

An **alpine planting mix** can be made by mixing two parts potting soil with one part sharp sand and a generous sprinkling of bonemeal.

Bonemeal

Sphagnum peatmoss is the best choice for creating hypertufa. Because the extraction of this material has an impact on the environment, use only a type from a managed source.

Garden Equipment

A **garden broom** should be used for cleaning soil from paving stones and brickwork.

A **garden fork** is used for preparing the ground for planting. It is useful for breaking up any large clods of earth.

Garden gloves are useful when handling rocks, or even soil, when it is essential to protect the hands. Tough gardening gloves are ideal.

A **garden trowel** is needed for making small holes for planting.

Use a **garden hose** for filling the water tank in the bubble fountain project and for watering larger areas with a sprinkler attachment.

A **rake** is used to prepare the ground for planting. Draw it backward and forward across the soil until a fine tilth and level ground is achieved.

Use a **spade** for mixing soil and cement, and for digging holes.

Use a **watering can** for watering plants after planting when they require a good drenching to remove any air pockets from around the roots, and to give them a good start. This is best done with a watering can or hose, with a fine spray attachment. Continue to water daily for two or three weeks after planting. The evening or early in the morning are the best times to water.

A **wheelbarrow** is essential for transporting soil and rockery material with the least effort.

Project Equipment and Tools

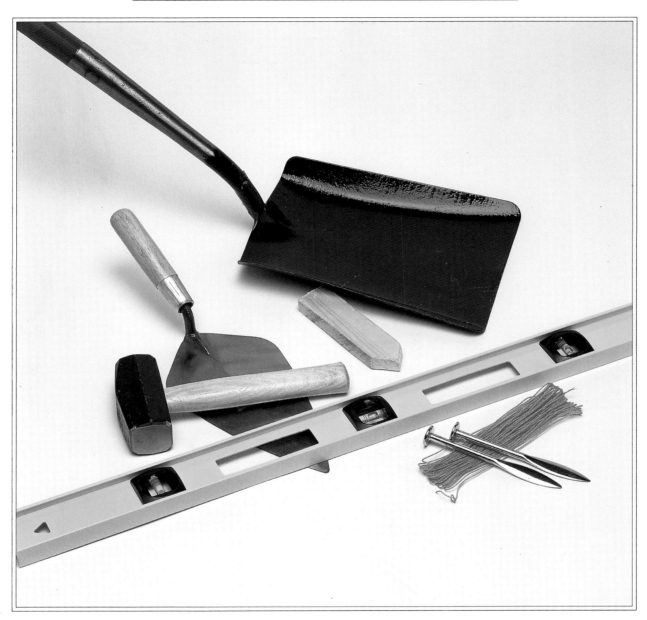

A **bricklayer's line** consists of two metal stakes and strong cord, and is used for insuring a straight line when laying bricks.

A **bricklayer's trowel** is essential for laying and pointing between bricks.

A **masonry chisel** is used for breaking corners off paving slabs.

An **electric drill** is used for making holes in the tufa in which to plant. An ordinary household drill is ideal.

Galvanized wire frames, used for reinforcing concrete and other building and construction tasks, are ideal for supporting cobblestones in bubble fountains.

The handle of a **brick hammer** is used to tap paving slabs level when laying them in place.

An **old paintbrush** is needed to paint PVA adhesive onto the side of an old-fashioned sink in the stone-sink project.

Use a **level** to make sure paving or brickwork is laid straight.

A **submersible water pump**, which is larger than your requirements, is best because the flow of water can then be adjusted accordingly.

A **water tank**, 20 inches deep by 26 inches diameter, made of plastic or fiberglass, such as those usually used in lofts or attics, is needed for the bubble fountain project.

ROCK OUTCROP

*T*his rock garden is designed to simulate an outcrop of rock, and will look most natural in an area where this phenomenon occurs naturally. It is part of an overall scheme, but a simple design of this size would make a fine feature on its own, perhaps with a wall or fence as a backdrop. The front of the rock garden could be combined with a scree bed or rock pavement.

The Plants

Here green-, yellow-, and variegated-leaf sedums and saxifrages form neat mounds with pink, red, white, and yellow flowers in spring and summer, while a juniper, a pale blue-flowered rosemary, and the rosettes of a house-leek provide low-growing, evergreen foliage. The delightful flowers of dianthus, lewisia, oxalis, and primroses in white, pink, and red shades contrast with the dark blue flowers of the veronica.

1
Saxifraga "White Pixie"

3
2 Sedum acre var. *aureum*

4
Saxifraga "Hi-Ace"

5
2 Saxifraga "Peter Pan"

2 *Sedum album* "Coral Carpet"

8 *Dianthus* "La Bourboule Albus"

12 *Sempervivum tectorum* (Houseleek)

6
Lewisia cotyledon hybrids

7
Rosmarinus officinalis "Severn Sea"

9
Saxifraga "Cloth of Gold"

10
Juniperus communis "Barton"

Materials

Alpine planting mix (see page 7) • Selected rockery stone in a variety of sizes • Garden trowel • Bricklayer's trowel • Heavy-duty gloves

Flowering Season

April to May.

2 *Veronica peduncularis* "Georgia Blue"

2 *Primula denticulata alba*

Oxalis adenophylla

2 *Primula rosea grandiflora*

Planting Plan

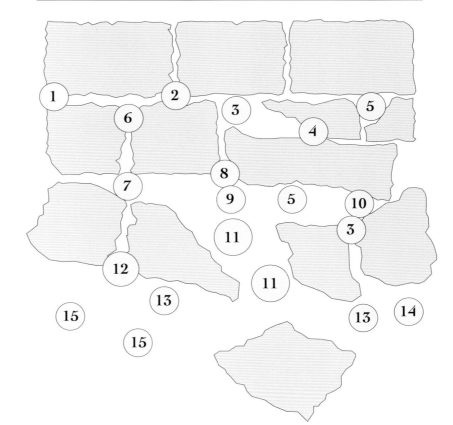

1. In certain areas, rock strata come to the surface, and it is this naturally occurring outcrop that is the origin of the garden rockery. When creating a rock garden of this nature, try to create something which simulates this and looks as natural as possible. This style of rock garden should be considered in an area where outcrops occur naturally, so it will appear truly natural, but careful positioning of stones will also create a suitably natural effect.

2. The stones used for this project may be too large to move comfortably. Use rounded fence stakes or wooden boards as runners to move them around.

3. Install the larger stones at the back, always trying to create an effect which simulates rock on the side of a mountain or outcrop. For strata appearing at the surface, like that shown in step 1, angle the stone at 45 degrees. It is important that the same angle is used throughout. Before placing a stone, look at the strata lines in the stone, and try to make these parallel throughout the arrangement.

4. When placing the stones, make sure that enough space is created between and around them for planting the alpines and rock plants.

5. Generally, alpines grow in well-drained, loose, stony areas on the side of mountains. It is essential, where possible, to simulate this, so backfill each planting space with drainage material, such as broken bricks, stones, and gravel.

CARE

Very little care is needed. Remove any flower heads after flowering.

6. Carefully fill each pocket with alpine planting mixture, slowly consolidating the mixture into any nooks or crannies by stopping periodically and firming well.

7. Following the Planting Plan, lay the plants out in their final position before planting. Remove each plant from its plastic pot by inverting it and gently squeezing the outside of the container. When removed from the pot, gently tease out the roots for planting. Dig a hole large enough for each plant, using your hand or a garden trowel.

8. Lewisias are perfectly frost-hardy, but detest winter moisture sitting in the crown of their leaves. To overcome this, they are best planted at an angle in the rock to allow rainwater to drain away.

9. After planting, spread pea-size pebbles, gravel or stone chips around the plants. This not only looks good, but also improves the drainage and reduces any "splash back" from heavy rain, which can soil the leaves of the tiny plants.

10. When completed, remove any loose soil from the rocks. If planted in the spring, the rock outcrop will soon mature, looking well-established by the end of its first summer.

ROCK PAVEMENT

In some cases, rock outcrops that appear at ground level, creating an interesting pattern, are flat enough to walk over. This variation of a scree bed has been designed to appear like one of these outcrops, is one of the best ways of

displaying alpine plants, and makes an interesting feature that could be incorporated into most garden designs. One approach is to regard the area as a dry riverbed with stepping stones across it.

The Plants

Mat- and rosette-forming saxifrages and an antennaria provide pink, white, red, and yellow flowers in spring and summer. Dwarf blue and white columbines combine with pink dianthus, erodium, cranesbills, primrose-yellow rockroses, lilac phlox, and purple and white pasqueflowers. The silvery blue foliage of blue fescue grass and the black grass-like *Ophiopogon*, with the thistle-like foliage and pink and white flower spikes of morina, provide a contrast in shape and color.

2 *Geranium cinereum "Ballerina"*

3 *Festuca glauca* (Blue fescue)

4 *Dianthus "Fusilier"*

6 *Pulsatilla vulgaris alba* (Pasqueflower)

10 *Saxifraga "Peter Pan"*

11 *Erodium reichardii*

16 *Pulsatilla vulgaris* (Pasqueflower)

1 *2 Ophiopogon planiscapus "Nigrescens"*

5 *Saxifraga x edithiae "Bridget"*

7 *Antennaria microphylla*

8 *Phlox subulata "Emerald Cushion Blue"*

9 *Aquilegia alpina* (Alpine columbine)

12 *Saxifraga "Schwefelblute"* (Flowers of sulphur)

13 *Morina longifolia*

14 *Saxifraga moschata "Cloth of Gold"*

15 *2 Helianthemum "Wisley Primrose"*

Planting Plan

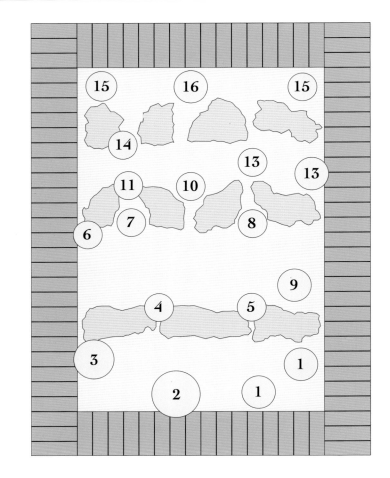

Flowering Season

Early spring to early summer.

Materials

Alpine planting mix (see page 7) •
90 bricks • Bricklayer's line •
Bricklayer's trowel • Lean mix (see
page 5) • Brick hammer • Mulching
mat • Selected rockery stone • Spade •
Level • Garden trowel

CARE

The occasional neatening to remove
any dead foliage or flower heads is all
that should be needed.

1. First mark out the pattern, then dig
out a trench about 9 inches wide and
6 inches deep. Line the excavation with
2 inches of lean mix.

2. Lay bricks in the pattern shown,
using a level to keep them straight and
a bricklayer's line to maintain a straight
line. Prepare the soil in the base of the
excavation by spreading a 2 inch layer
of sharp sand across the surface and
incorporating it into the top spade's
depth of soil.

3. To keep weeds down, lay the
mulching mat across the surface and
cover with a 4 inch layer of alpine
planting mix. Place selected stones in
the pattern desired. Here, we are
simulating strata rising to the surface
and have been careful to follow the
contours in the stone.

4. Lay the plants out in their position for planting.

5. Some plants will look at their best if growing in cracks between the stones. Remove the plant from its pot and squeeze the rootball to a shape where it will fit easily into the allocated space.

6. Before planting, tease out the roots from the rootball to make sure that the plant grows away well. Cut a cross in the mulching mat and plant through it.

7. Spread a layer of pea-size pebbles or fine gravel across the surface, being careful to cover the soil completely.

8. Lift any spreading plants, and gently push the stones underneath.

9. The pebbles look good and will keep the soil cool around the roots, something which many alpines appreciate. They also protect the small leaves from "splash back" in heavy rainstorms, an action which soils them and can cause some damage.

10. A mature scree bed makes an attractive garden feature. It is the perfect way to grow alpines.

BUBBLE FOUNTAIN

*F*lowing water, perhaps cascading over a rock, pouring from an overturned urn, or simply bubbling over stones will enhance any garden. This project shows how to make a basic bubble fountain, the perfect addition to any scree bed or small rock garden.

As a variation, a hole could be drilled through the center of a large rock, and the fountain pipe extended through it so water bubbles up through the hole and cascades down the sides of the rock. This could be incorporated into any kind of rock garden to give the appearance of an emerging spring.

Materials

Cobblestones • Selected stones •
2 engineering bricks • 1 extension pipe
• 2 galvanized wire frames,
30 inches square • Hose
• Spade or shovel • Level
• Submersible water pump,
216 gallons per hour
• Water tank, 20 inches deep by
26 inches diameter

CARE

Treat the water with an algicide to make sure algae does not collect on the stones.

The Plants

The big round leaves of heartleaf bergenia, tall variegated iris, glaucous gray parahebe with its dainty blue flowers, a waving grass, and a spreading, yellow-foliaged, dwarf yew provide all-year-round contrast and color around the bubbling water.

Iris foetidissima "Variegata"

Parahebe catarractae

Bergenia cordifolia "Purpurea"

Taxus baccata "Repens Aurea"

Pennisetum alopecuroides

Planting Plan

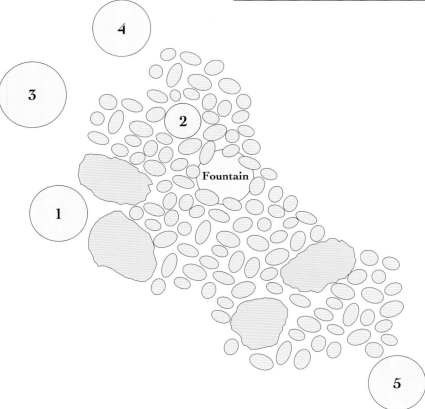

1. Dig a hole large enough for the water tank.

2. The hole should be a little larger than the tank to allow room to work.

3. Using a level, make sure the tank is straight. Adjust by adding or removing soil from the base of the excavation. When positioned correctly, fill with water, still using the level to make sure the tank remains straight.

4. To make sure that the water pump is at the right level, place two engineering bricks in the base of the tank.

5. Place the water pump on the bricks. Make sure the extension pipe extends above the water level.

6. Place one of the wire frames across the tank, insuring the extension pipe protrudes in the center.

7. To make sure the smaller cobblestones do not fall through the mesh, place the second wire frame at right angles to the first. Place the cobblestones loosely over the frame.

8. The water pump will require power. This is best supplied through a plastic conduit from the house.

9. Adjust the flow of water using a combination of the faucet on the pump and cobblestones piled around the end of the pipe. Be patient, it can take some time to get the flow just right.

10. Add selected large, round cobblestones for effect. These are sometimes referred to as "ostrich eggs."

11. Push pea-size pebbles up around the cobblestones to integrate the bubble fountain with the surrounding scree bed.

12. Grassy and spiky leaves are a good choice to accompany a bubble fountain and cobblestones. Here, we have planted *Iris foetidissima* "Variegata."

13. Low-growing alpines look good cascading over cobblestones.

14. Bubble fountains are perfect as an addition to a scree bed.

15. Bubble fountains are a versatile garden feature, and can even be incorporated into a small bed close to a patio area.

GRAHAM A PAVEY

RYL NOWELL'S GARDEN . RHS CHELSEA FLOWER SHOW

16. When the basic fountain has been installed, there are an infinite number of variations for the fountain, from drilled boulders to various containers of all shapes and sizes.

STONE SINK GARDEN

*B*efore porcelain came into common use, natural stone was carved to create sinks, and these old, worn stone containers, so treasured by gardeners, are the perfect choice for period and country gardens. They can look good on each side of a farmhouse doorway.

Materials

A stone sink,
24 inches x 16 inches x 6 inches
• Garden trowel • Pebbles
• Alpine planting mix (see page 7)
• Small piece of rock • Stone chips

CARE

Remove any dead leaves or flower heads, as necessary.

Flowering Season

Early to late spring.

The Plants

Evergreen mats of foliage are provided by an androsace, a rock pink, phlox, saxifrages, and red houseleeks, while a dwarf juniper provides an upright feature. The delightful pink flowers of the androsace, dwarf pinks, phlox, and saxifrage, the blue of *Anemone blanda*, and a yellow saxifrage glow through-out the spring.

(1)

Juniperus communis "Compressa"

(3)

Saxifraga x *elisabethae* "Primrose Dame"

(5)

Saxifraga "Silver Cushion"

(6)

Sempervivum "Black Prince" (Houseleek)

(7)

Phlox subulata "Temiskaming"

(8)

Anemone blanda

(2) *Dianthus* "Pike's Pink"

(4) *Androsace sempervivoides*

Planting Plan

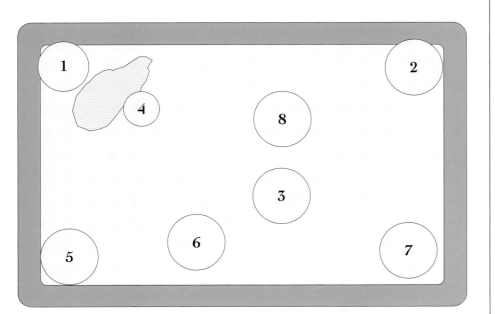

1. Old stone troughs are often already covered with patinas of lichen and moss, all of which add to their attraction.

2. Place some crockery shards over the drainage hole, and line the base of the sink with a layer of pebbles. Room is limited, so this cannot be too deep. Fill with alpine planting mixture up to the rim, and consolidate well.

3. Place a small piece of rock close to one corner for effect. This could be anything, but tufa would be a good choice.

4. Remove each plant from its pot by inverting it and gently squeezing the sides. Tease out the roots from the rootball before planting.

5. After planting, spread a layer of stone chips around the plants. Make sure that all areas are covered, lifting any spreading plants to push the stone chips underneath.

6. The plants in the final planted-up container will soon be well-established.

SINK GARDEN

Genuine stone sinks are popular containers for alpines, but are hard to find. However, this old glazed porcelain sink can be converted to make an effective and charming alternative.

Flowering Season

Spring

Materials

Alpine planting mix (see page 7)
• An old glazed sink, about 11 inches x 24 inches wide x 18 inches side width
• Bricklayer's trowel
• Crockery shards • Old paintbrush
• PVA-based adhesive or bonding agent • Sharp sand, cement, and sphagnum peatmoss, strained and lumps removed

The Plants

Bright pink thrift and alpine pinks mingle with brilliant blue trumpet-shaped gentians, unusual pink-and-white-flowered alpine phlox, white saxifrage and phlox, yellow sisyrinchium, and saxifrage. The silver, blue, and green evergreen foliage of the dwarf juniper, thrift, pinks, gentian, saxifrages, and grass-like sisyrinchium provide all-year-round charm.

Armeria maritima "Dusseldorfer Stolz"

Saxifraga x elisabethae "Primrose Dame"

(7) *Phlox subulata* "Kimono"

(3) *Sisyrinchium californicum*

(4) *Saxifraga* "Whitehills"

(8) *Dianthus* "La Bourboule"

(9) *Phlox subulata* "Maischnee"

Juniperus communis "Compressa"

Gentiana acaulis

Planting Plan

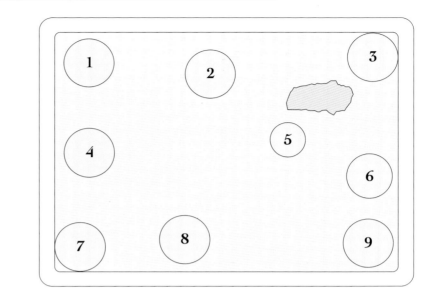

1. Clean the sink thoroughly and leave it to dry. Score the surface with a glass cutter, file, or tile cutter to make a good contact for the adhesive and hypertufa mixture.

2. Give the sink two coats of adhesive, leaving both to completely dry before progressing. A third and final coat should be brushed on immediately before step 3.

3. Mix enough hypertufa to cover the sink, using 1 part sand, 1 part cement, and 2 parts peatmoss. Mix the sand and cement thoroughly, and then add the peatmoss, which should be moistened first. Mix thoroughly and add a little water at a time, until the mixture is sufficiently moist to adhere to the sides of the sink.

4. Spread a fairly thin layer of hypertufa onto the sink (approximately 1 inch), and make sure this covers over the top edge and down inside the container. Before the mixture dries, square off the rim to simulate a smooth stone edge.

CARE

The gentian needs an acid soil, so make sure only rainwater is used when watering.

5. When the initial hardening has occurred, allow the trough to dry slowly by covering with plastic or damp burlap for a day or two. Line the base of the sink with a generous layer of crockery shards for drainage.

6. Position the plants for planting. Care should be taken in selecting plants suitable for a sink garden to make sure that they are not going to outgrow the space available.

7. Prepare each plant for planting by teasing the roots from the rootball.

9. Place the finished container in its final position, supported on bricks to aid drainage even more. The project will soon develop if planted in the spring, and will be well-established by the end of the first summer.

8. After planting, spread a layer of stone chips or horticultural gravel over the whole surface of the container. Lift the edge of any trailing plants and push the gravel underneath. This mulch will help to protect the plants and create a friendly environment for them.

10. Set aside an area in the garden devoted to these stone sinks. A graveled area as part of a patio is the perfect place, where an odd number, perhaps three or five, can be set out in a group.

BILL SHAW

TUFA GARDEN

Tufa is a very light material used to create walls in conservatories and ferneries, and on the inside walls of courtyards and cloister gardens.

Large chunks of tufa embedded into a scree bed and planted with various alpines make an unusual garden feature that always attracts attention.

Flowering Season

There are odd splashes of color through the year, but the main flowering season will be late spring through to mid-summer.

Materials

Alpine planting mix (see page 7)
• 2 pieces of tufa • Electric drill
• Large-diameter drill bit • Teaspoon

CARE
Virtually none. Keep well watered in dry weather.

The Plants

The silver, green, and purple sedum grows low, and tumbles over rocks and ground wherever it is planted, and the tiny alpine erinus will happily seed itself around, popping up in the tiniest cracks between rocks to show its bright pink flowers. In contrast, the houseleek, with its tiny white hairs, gives the impression it is covered with a spider's web. An androsace, rock pinks, and a saxifrage provide colorful pink and yellow flowers.

1 *2 Dianthus "Pink Jewel"*

2 *Androsace sarmentosa*

3 *Sedum spathulifolium "Cape Blanco"*

4 *Saxifraga x apiculata*

6 *Sempervivum arachnoideum*

5 *Erinus alpinus "Dr Hahnle"*

Planting Plan

1. Before making any holes, decide where your plants would look best. The patina in the stone can be attractive, and you may want to leave it exposed.

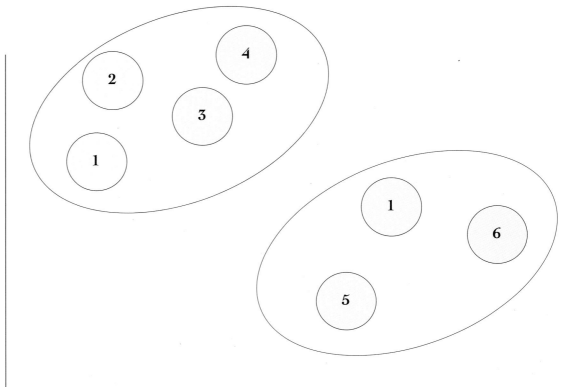

2. An extra pair of hands will be needed for this step. After you have decided where the holes are to be drilled, hold the stone firmly, using the extra pair of hands.

3. Drill a hole sufficiently large enough to take the rootball of the plant to be used (this can be squashed down to fit, so do not make the hole too large). The hole can be made with an old screwdriver, but this is more time-consuming.

4. Remove the tufa dust with the teaspoon. The dust is useful and should be incorporated into the alpine planting mix.

5. Backfill the hole with alpine planting mix. Not all alpines are suitable for growing in tufa, so consult a reliable alpine nursery for advice.

6. Remove the plant from its pot by inverting it and gently squeezing the sides. Squash the rootball to make sure it fits comfortably into the hole; if necessary, remove some of the soil – do not be afraid, the plants are quite tough.

7. The plant must be consolidated. Do this by firming with the handle end of the teaspoon, adding more alpine planting mix, as necessary. When planted, a gentle tug should not dislodge it. The roots of the alpine will invade the tufa itself in time, and will live quite happily in a soil-free environment.

8. After the tufa is planted up, one-third of it should be buried in the ground (or soft sand). The capillary action of the tufa will then draw water and nutrients from the ground below.

ALPINES IN PAVING

A good way of deciding where to grow a plant in a garden is to look at how it grows in its native environment. Alpines like to grow in holes in rocks and among loose stones, and these would be perfect choices for softening a paved area, particularly a patio.

One of the rules of garden design states that the size of the patio should be equal to one-third the height of the house to the eaves. In some cases the paved area can often look too large and unwelcoming, so growing plants between the cracks in the paving helps soften the area.

1 — *2 Acaena* "Blue Haze" (New Zealand burr)

2 — *Thymus* "Doone Valley"

3 — *Chamaemelum nobile* "Treneague"

The Plants

Here, delightfully colored and often aromatic foliage is used to create a patchwork of evergreen underfoot. From its solid mat of ground-covering, steel-blue foliage, New Zealand burr produces fuzzy, round reddish-brown flowers, and the little alpine alchemilla has the crinkled foliage and lime green flowers of its larger cousin – lady's mantle. The aromatic chamomile, used to create chamomile lawns, the Corsican mint, and two thymes – one with green-and-gold leaves – all have aromatic leaves, especially when crushed. The evergreen phlox provides a splash of color with its crimson flowers in late spring and early summer.

4 — *Phlox douglasii* "Red Admiral"

5 — *Thymus herba-barona* (Caraway thyme)

6 — *Alchemilla alpina*

7 — *Mentha requienii* (Corsican mint)

CARE

An occasional trim of the plants will keep them compact.

Planting Plan

Flowering Season

The plants in this scheme have been chosen primarily for their attractive ground-covering foliage, but the main flourish is in late spring to midsummer.

Materials

Alpine planting mix (see page 7)
• Bricklayer's trowel • Chisel
• Rubble • Lean mix (see page 5)
• Brick hammer • Gloves • Spade
• Level

1. Mark out the area, and dig out the soil to a depth suitable for accepting the layer of rubble and lean mix.

2. Break off the corners of the paving slabs where plants are to be planted. Mark the piece of slab to be removed by gently tapping the chisel with the brick hammer all the way around the piece.

3. Give the corner one sharp tap with the brick hammer, and it should break off. If it does not, then repeat step 2. If the corner does not come away cleanly, it will not matter, because the plants will cover any mistakes.

4. Line the base of the excavation with rubble, and backfill with a lean mix of sand and cement. Lay the paving stones using a level and the brick hammer handle to make sure the whole paved area is straight and firm.

5. Brush alpine planting mix into the spaces and cracks left in the paving.

6. Lay the plants out where they are to be planted. The plants chosen here are all ground-hugging, many of which are aromatic when stepped on.

7. Remove each plant from its container and reshape the rootball before planting into its position. Use the alpine planting mix to consolidate each plant.

8. After planting, the plants will soon begin to cover the paving slabs. In time, the paving will change dramatically, covered with a mat of many different colors.

DRY STONE WALL

*S*tone walls have been used for centuries in Europe to section off areas of land, and have become the homes for many plants usually found on cliffs and in stony places. This project looks at creating a dry stone wall for growing alpines. Building a dry stone wall is a fairly simple way of making a dramatic improvement to the look of your garden. As a retaining wall, it will have much more impact than a characterless concrete structure. By making a feature of the walls, we can create a strong addition to the garden instead of something simply utilitarian.

The Plants

In early spring, the flowers of dwarf daffodils, primroses, saxifrages, and Siberian squills bring a sparkle to nooks and crannies. Pink and white saxifrages, and pink phlox bloom, many continuing into the summer to be joined by large pink rockroses, give a colorful display among mats of evergreen foliage and rosettes of houseleeks and yellow sedums.

Flowering Season

Spring and summer.

Materials

Alpine planting mix (see page 7)
• Cement • Drainage material
• Garden trowel • Spade • Dry stone-walling material

(2)

2 Scilla sibirica (Siberian squill)

(3)

Saxifraga "Silver Cushion"

(4)

Saxifraga "White Pixie"

(5)

2 Narcissus "Minnow"

(6)

Phlox subulata "Alexander's Surprise"

(7)

3 Primula vulgaris (Primrose)

(9)

2 Sedum acre var. *aureum*

(8) *Helianthemum* "Georgeham" (Rockrose)

(1) *Saxifraga* "Whitehills"

(10) *Sempervivum tectorum* (Houseleek)

Planting Plan

1. Make sure the ground is carefully prepared and consolidated to form a solid base. Bed down the first layer of stones, selecting them to achieve a good "interlock." Fill the spaces between the stones with large-grade drainage material.

2. Place the second layer on top of the first. Look for a solid base, and use small pieces of stones to keep the larger ones level.

3. Build the layers up to the desired level. Keep the wall low, no more than about 24 inches high and backfill with drainage material to within 6 inches of the top.

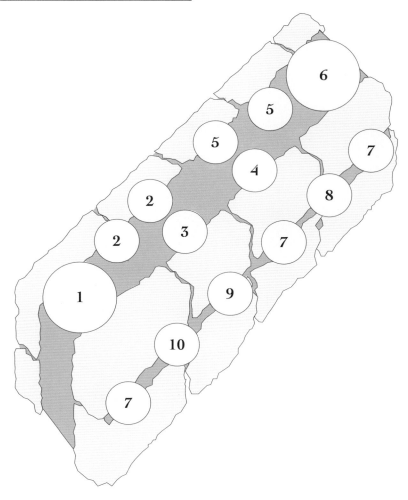

4. Fill holes with alpine planting mix, and consolidate well.

5. When completed, lay the plants out in their positions for planting.

6. Remove plants from pots by inverting and gently squeezing the sides. Tease out roots from the rootball before planting.

CARE

Remove dead leaves and flower heads from plants, as necessary.

The structure should be inspected each spring, and any winter damage repaired.

7. A layer of stone chips, to match the natural stone, may be spread around the plants on top of the wall.

8. The finished wall will make the perfect addition to any garden. In time, these stones will weather down and become colored by moss and lichens.

SCREE BED

*M*ost true alpines grow in scree – loose stones and shale on slopes high up on a mountainside, so this scree bed is an ideal and attractive way of growing alpines. It is best placed close to the house, perhaps between the patio and the lawn. An expanded area could have stepping stones incorporated and laid in a pattern, to add interest and allow a passage through the bed.

The Plants

Spreading mats and mounds of aubretia, armeria, and thyme are dotted with their purple and white flowers. Contrasting forms of silvery gray-green foliage of artemisia, verbascum, pinks, and blue corydalis combine with a yellow alpine hypericum and the pink, fluffy, round flower heads of thrift and chives to create a charming picture.

1

Artemisia schmidtiana "Nana"

2

2 Verbascum olympicum

3

Corydalis caespitosa

4

Thymus "Doone Valley"

5

Sagina subulata "Aurea"

6

Hypericum aegypticum

7

Dianthus "Fusilier"

8

Armeria juniperifolia (Thrift)

9

Allium schoenoprasum (Chives)

10

Aubretia deltoidea

Planting Plan

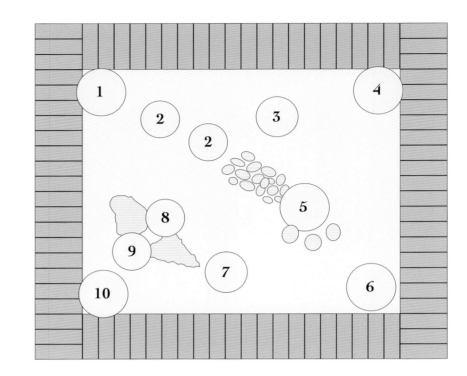

Flowering Season

Early spring to early summer.

Materials

Alpine planting mix (see page 7)
• 90 bricks • 2 small rocks • 3 large
and several small cobblestones
• Pea-size pebbles • Bricklayer's line
• Bricklayer's trowel • Lean mix
(see page 5) • Brick hammer
• Mulching mat • Spade • Level
• Garden trowel

1. Prepare the ground carefully,
incorporating sharp sand in the form of
a 2 inch thick surface layer, dug into
the top to a spade's depth. Smooth the
area over with a rake or garden fork.

2. Mark out the pattern and dig out a
trench, about 8½ inches wide and
6 inches deep.

3. Line the excavation with 2 inches of
lean mix. Lay bricks in the pattern
shown, using a level to keep them straight
and a bricklayer's line to maintain a
straight line. Make sure each brick is
firmly laid into the lean mix.

CARE

Neaten occasionally to remove any dead
foliage or flower heads. The artemisia
should be cut back hard each spring to
encourage regrowth.

4. Make sure bricks are laid flat and in a straight line throughout, because it is important that the square shape is maintained in the completed design.

5. Lay a mulch mat across the soil to help keep moisture in the soil in hot weather and reduce the growth of weeds. Cover with a 4 inch layer of alpine planting mix, and top with a layer of pebbles, level to the top of the bricks.

6. Incorporate rockery stone and loose cobblestones to create an attractive effect. Try to make it look as natural as possible, with the stones appearing as if there is much more below the surface. Lay the plants out in their positions for planting.

7. Before planting, prepare each plant by gently teasing out the roots from the rootball. Scrape back the pebbles, make a cross-shaped cut in the mulching mat, and insert the plant through it.

GRAHAM A PAVEY

8. A "desert" scree arrangement
demonstrates that the scree bed need
not be restricted to temperate zones.
The plants here will mature over
several months.

ALPINES IN A STRAWBERRY POT

This type of container is perfect for growing alpines, especially where space is limited. The more robust rock plants, which would otherwise invade the space of neighboring plants in a rock garden or scree bed, can be grown. Display on a wall or step to give these plants room to cascade.

Flowering Season

Summer

Materials

1 strawberry pot, 15 inches x 6½ inches • Crockery shards • Alpine planting mix (see page 7)

CARE

The strawberry planter may be placed in sun or partial shade. Water every evening during hot summer weather, and once a month in the winter. The gentian will require acid soil, so make sure the soil remains peaty and use only rainwater to avoid raising the pH. An occasional "haircut" for the plants will be beneficial.

The Plants

The variegated, green and yellow foliage of trailing and spreading plants is dotted with sparkling yellow, pink, and blue flowers in summer, and topped with the vibrant blue flowers of the gentian.

3

Gentiana septemfida

1

Drosanthemum hispidum

4

Parahebe catarractae

2

2 Lysimachia nummularia "Aureum"
(Creeping jennie)

5

2 Arabis fernandi-coburgi "Variegata"

Planting Plan

1. Line the base of the container with crockery shards to aid drainage.

Top Layer

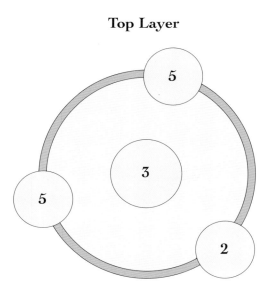

Lower Layer

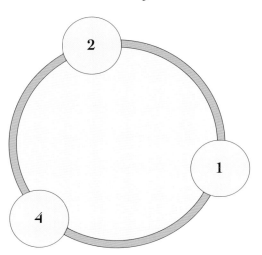

2. Add alpine planting mixture up to the first level of holes, making sure it is well consolidated.

3. Decide where each plant is to go before starting to plant.

4. Remove each plant from its plastic container by inverting it and squeezing the sides. Gently squash up the roots, and insert plants through the holes.

5. Add more alpine planting mixture, firming gently, and bring the level up to the second layer of holes.

6. Plant up the second layer of holes and add more planting mixture. Finish the container by planting the final plant – the gentian. Top with a mulch of sand or fine gravel, which will enhance the plant's leaves and blue flowers.

7. The container will quickly fill out and can be displayed immediately. Position on a wall or stone step to allow the plants to cascade down the sides of the planter.

ALPINE BOWL

*T*his miniature garden is perfect where space is limited and little room exists for creating a rock garden. It makes an attractive addition to a small patio, balcony, or cool sunroom.

Flowering Season

Summer

Materials

A raised terra-cotta bowl, 20 inches x 7½ inches • Crockery shards • Alpine planting mix (see page 7) • Selected stones

CARE

The alpine bowl may be placed in sun or partial shade. Water every evening during hot summer weather, and once a month in the winter. The soil should be acid, and only rainwater should be used to avoid raising the pH.

The Plants

These delightful little rock-garden and alpine plants in a terra-cotta bowl make a perfect miniature garden in even the smallest space.

1

Saponaria x *olivana* (Soapwort)

2

Gentiana macaulayi "Praecox"

3

Cyclamen hederifolium album

4

2 Erodium x *variabile* "Roseum"

5

Ononis fruticosa

6

Erodium x *variabile* "Album"

Planting Plan

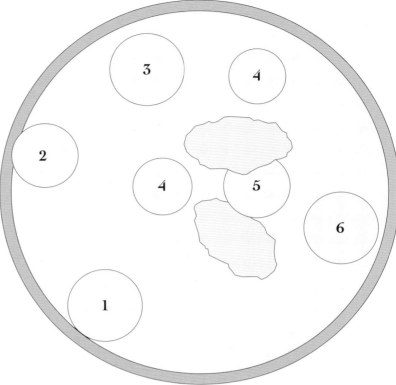

1. Line the base of the bowl with crockery shards to aid drainage.

2. Add alpine planting mixture, bringing it up to about 1½ inches from the rim. Make sure it is firmed and well consolidated.

3. Position selected stones. Make sure they are large enough to sit securely in the planting mix. These are limestone, but a good alternative would be tufa.

4. Remove plants from their containers and gently tease out the roots before introducing them to the container.

47

5. Plant up around the stones first to make sure the plants remain firmly in place.

6. Complete planting before spreading horticultural gravel across the top of the planting mixture, working it in around and under the plants. This will help to keep the roots damp and cool, and will enhance the plants' appearance.

7. The final container can be used immediately.